SBC Helldiver

in action

By Thomas E. Doll

**Color By Don Greer &
Tom Tullis**

**Illustrated by Joe
Sewell**

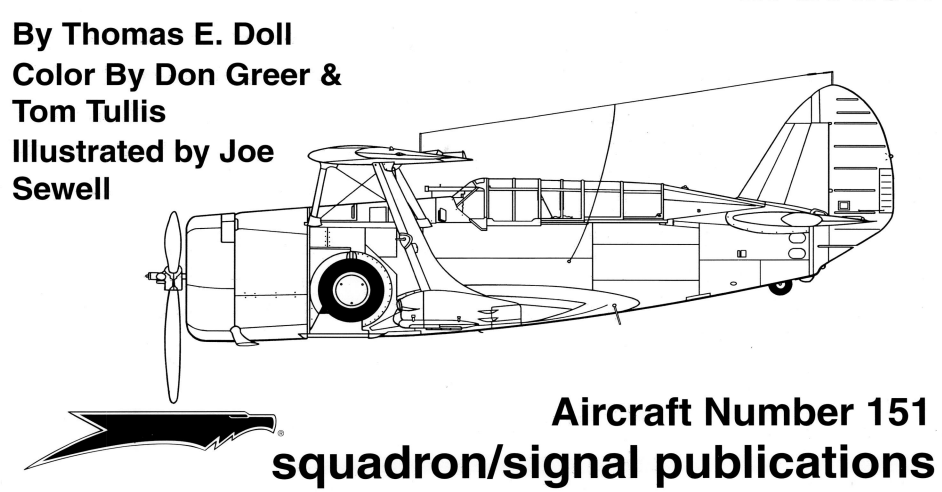

Aircraft Number 151

squadron/signal publications

A SBC-4 Helldiver of VMO-151 flies over the jungles of Samoa during 1942. The squadron was the last front-line Marine Corps unit to fly the Helldiver.

Dedication

This book is dedicated to that dauntless band of pre-Second World War amateur photographers who loved airplanes and taking pictures of them. These young men did not just shoot at random, they had a strict set of guidelines to insure that their photographs would exhibit the highest quality possible.

Today, almost sixty-five years later, this group can be justifiably proud of their record. Although the original organization, the International Amateur Aircraft Photo Exchange, I.A.A.P .E., only lasted from 1930 to 1935, it set the standard for all who came after. If it were not for them, the pages of this book and countless others, would lack high quality photographs of the aircraft from so very long ago.

Fred E. Bamberger	Peter M. Bowers	Henry Clark
Lee Enich	Arthur B. Green	Ben H. Heinowitz
Donald F. Kauer	William T. Larkins	Howard Levy
Harold G. Martin	John C. Mitchell	Harold Nolen
Boardman C. Reed	Frank Shertzer	Warren D. Shipp
Emil Strasser	William L. Swisher	Harry Thorell
Gordon S. Williams	William F. Yeager	

Acknowledgements

A heartfelt thank you to the following individuals who gave so much of their time and effort during the preparation of this book. I will never be able to adequately express my gratitude to them for the unselfish assistance they extended to me.

To Dave Lucabaugh for his invaluable work in providing historical data and photographs on two of his favorite aircraft. To Bill Swisher, for his fine photos and superb squadron organizational chart idea and research. To Bob Cressmen who researched and located valuable information on the activities of VMO-151. Others include:

Owen Darcey	Bude Donato
Harry Gann	M/SGT W.F.Gemeinhardt, USMC. Ret.
Berkley R. Jackson	Clay Jansson
CAPT Donald Kirkpatrick, USN, Ret.	David Steinbacher
CAPT Charles E. Roemer, USN, Ret.	Joseph H. Weathers, Jr.
USMC Historical Branch	USN/National Archives
Hill Goodspeed, National Museum of Naval Aviation	Ardy Jahan, Printec

If you have any photographs of aircraft, armor, soldiers or ships of any nation, particularly wartime snapshots, why not share them with us and help make Squadron/Signal's books all the more interesting and complete in the future. Any photograph sent to us will be copied and the original returned. The donor will be fully credited for any photos used. Please send them to:

Squadron/Signal Publications, Inc.
1115 Crowley Drive
Carrollton, TX 75011-5010

Если у вас есть фотографии самолётов, вооружения, солдат или кораблей любой страны, особенно, снимки времён войны, поделитесь с нами и помогите сделать новые книги издательства Эскадрон/Сигнал ещё интереснее. Мы переснимем ваши фотографии и вернём оригиналы. Имена приславших снимки будут сопровождать все опубликованные фотографии. Пожалуйста, присылайте фотографии по адресу:

Squadron/Signal Publications, Inc.
1115 Crowley Drive
Carrollton, TX 75011-5010

軍用機、装甲車両、兵士、軍艦などの写真を所持しておられる方は いらっしゃいませんか？どの国のものでも結構です。作戦中に撮影されたものが特に良いのです。Squadron/Signal社の出版する刊行物において、このような写真は内容を一層充実し、興味深くすることができます。当方にお送り頂いた写真は、複写の後お返しいたします。出版物中に写真を使用した場合は、必ず提供者のお名前を明記させて頂きます。お写真は下記にご送付ください。

Squadron/Signal Publications, Inc.
1115 Crowley Drive
Carrollton, TX 75011-5010

This SBC-4 was assigned to the Naval Reserve Air Base (NRAB) at Oakland, California. The fuselage stripe and cowling were in White. (W.T. Larkins)

Introduction

During the late-1930's Curtiss SBC-3 and SBC-4 dive-bombers, operating from Fleet carriers, participated in the early development of United States Naval Aviation. They helped develop the tactics and doctrine of the art of dive-bombing from the time of their entry into Fleet service until 1941, when newer and more capable aircraft began to replace them. As the Navy carried out its yearly schedule of exercises and training, interspersed with upkeep periods, culminating in the annual large scale war games, or "Fleet Problems," the SBCs took their place alongside other aircraft types in which Navy and Marine pilots and aircrewmen learned their demanding trade. Those operations were not conducted without cost; however, and occasionally aircraft (and sometimes men) would be lost at sea, reminding those who went to sea in carriers that theirs was an operation just as dangerous in peacetime as it was in war.

Forever known as the last combat biplane flown by the United States Navy and Marine Corps, the Curtiss SBC-4 scout-bomber can trace its beginning back to the Curtiss XF12C-1, a two-seat fighter developed during 1932/33.

The XF12C-1 did not resemble the SBC-4, but if there had not been a XF12C-1, there would not have been a SBC-4 dive-bomber.

On 30 June 1932, the Bureau of Aeronautics (BuAer) ordered three fighter aircraft prototypes from the Curtiss, Douglas and Vought aircraft companies. The following year all three designs were in the air going through their paces in hopes of winning a production contract. Douglas and Vought entered bi-plane designs while the Curtiss entry was a parasol winged monoplane. They all were two seat fighters as per the BuAer's directive, but the Curtiss prototype featured retractable landing gear while the Douglas and Vought aircraft had fixed landing gear. The XF12C-1 had full-span leading and trailing edge flaps, folding wings for carrier stowage and was built around the 625 hp Wright R-1510-92 Twin Whirlwind air-cooled radial engine. The Douglas and Vought designs used the 700 hp Pratt & Whitney R-1535-64 air-cooled radial.

The XF12C-1's performance was satisfactory, but not spectacular; however, this could also

The XF12C-1 featured full span leading edge slats, retractable landing gear and trailing edge flaps. (Curtiss via Peter Bowers)

be said of the aircraft's competition. By this time, the Navy was reconsidering the two place fighter concept and the XF12C-1 would be reconfigured for another role, that of scout-observation.

BuAer sent a letter to the Chief of the Bureau of Supplies and Accounts, dated 7 December 1933, which outlined the changes it wanted in order to modify the XF12C-1 to its new role under the designation XS4C-1. This directive was labeled Change No. 11 and included the following: Install a Wright SR1820F-3 engine (to be furnished by the government). Curtiss was to furnish and install new engine mounts, cowling and other materials necessary for the engine change; provide and install all parts necessary for carriage of a 500 pound bomb except the bomb displacement gear, which would be covered under a separate contract with BuOrd;.rework main fuel tank; furnish one fuel tank and test same in accordance with current Bureau specifications and redesign and construct new auxiliary fuel tank with new dump valve control. Construct one auxiliary tank and test in accordance with current Navy Department specifications. With these modifications complete, the Navy redesignated the aircraft as the XS4C-1; however, this designation was destined to be short lived. A month later the Navy decided to move the aircraft from the Scout-observation category to the Scout-bomber category and changed the designation to XSBC-1. The original Bureau number (BuNo), 9225, was retained.

The XS4C-1 probably did not have the new engine installed before the designation was changed. During this time period, BuAer began to seriously seek development of monoplane

The Curtiss XF12C-1 two seat fighter prototype on the ramp at the Curtiss factory on 29 July 1933. This aircraft was later modified and redesignated as the XS4C. (Curtiss via Peter Bowers)

The prototype also featured a folding wing to make the aircraft more compact for storage on carrier decks. It was re-engined with a 625 hp Wright RS1820F-3 radial engine and redsignated the XS4C-1. (Curtiss via Peter Bowers)

aircraft types to serve aboard the new carriers that were under construction. Prototypes of the Douglas TBD-1, Northrop BT-1 and Vought SB2U-1 all made their appearance during the mid-1930s. Of these two, the SB2U-1 and TBD would see combat during the early days of the Second World War.

The XSBC-1 entered into a concentrated series of tests during early 1934. The new Wright R-1820-80 air cooled radial engine gave the aircraft a top speed of 216 mph at 8,000 feet and a service ceiling of 24,000 feet. Routine testing and night flying tests, as a scout, were carried out, along with some dive-bombing tests. The dive-bombing tests paid specific attention to the operation of the wing slots and flaps. It was during this series of tests that the XSBC-1 was lost.

On 14 June 1934, shortly before 0600, in Buffalo, New York, the XSBC-1 took off from the Curtiss factory for a preliminary dive-bombing demonstration with a 500 pound bomb being carried on the centerline bomb rack. Two dives were made, one with a velocity of 260 mph and the other at 290 mph. Accelerations of 4Gs were also recorded. Inspections after the flight disclosed no evidence of damage or strain on the structure. The pilot, Paul Hovgard, reported a slight buffeting of the tail, but this was not considered serious.

The XSBC-1 resumed dive testing shortly after 0700. The third dive of the day was uneventful, but on the fourth dive, disaster struck the XSBC-1.

Cloud conditions were such that the dive was partly obscured from the ground. On the second dive of this flight, which was not seen by witnesses on the ground, an explosion was heard which, considered in conjunction with engine noise, indicated that the aircraft had only dived a short distance prior to being damaged. This fact was later confirmed by the pilot, who stated to the inspector that he had only entered the dive and that the speed was not yet as high as in the dives on the previous flight.

Paul Hovgard told the inspector that there were two explosions, one immediately after the other. He stated that the nose of the aircraft came up quickly to about horizontal and that the XSBC-1 began to spin slowly in this attitude. It was at this point that the pilot exited the aircraft. He jumped at about 12,000 feet and fell some distance before pulling his rip cord. In the jump the pilot suffered a broken right arm and right leg before landing. It was determined that he was struck by the tail section after he jumped. There was a slight laceration on his right hand which led the inspector to that conclusion. The pilot reported that the aircraft passed him and he noted that the horizontal stabilizer was folded upward alongside the verti-

The XSBC-1 on the ramp at the Curtiss factory. The aircraft retained its original BuNo, 9225, through two modification programs and three designation changes. (Curtiss via C. Jansson)

The XSBC-1 crashed on 14 June 1934, after a propeller blade seperated in a high speed dive. The pilot escaped with a broken arm and leg. (Thorell Aircraft Photos via Peter Bowers)

cal fin.

The aircraft crashed in a small open spot in the town of Lancaster, New York, about six miles from the Curtiss factory. The XSBC-1 came down in a. flat attitude and pancaked into the ground. Considering the violence connected with any aircraft crash, the XSBC-1 was in remarkably good condition. The wing appeared undamaged except for minor damage caused by the initial impact with the ground. The horizontal stabilizer was folded up on each side of the fuselage at an angle of about forty-five degrees and the forward beam on each side was broken about six inches outboard on each side of the fuselage. Part of the engine and engine mount were torn out. The fuselage bottom was crushed upward by the impact with the ground and by the unexploded bomb.

The engine was found about one mile from the aircraft. One propeller blade and hub were still with the engine. The other blade was found about two miles from where the engine landed and had broken off in the hub. The pilot landed about three miles from the aircraft, with his parachute, and was taken to Millard Fillmore Hospital in Buffalo by ambulance. The cause of the crash was determined to be the failure of a propeller blade, which let go, followed immediately by the engine and the breaking of the horizontal stabilizer from excessive vibration. The XSBC-1, two-seat scout bomber, was gone forever.

On 6 July 1934, Curtiss petitioned BuAer regarding the construction of a replacement aircraft for the XSBC-1. This proposal eliminated the folding wings and called for a complete redesign of the fuselage structure to provide for full metal monocoque construction in lieu of the previous combination of welded tubular steel and metal monocoque. An improvement in the cabin structure of the cockpits was proposed, including the installation of a streamlined rear folding turtledeck section.

Unlike the XSBC-1, the replacement would be a biplane and the single spar upper wing would not have leading edge slots, but the lower wing would be fitted with full span flaps. The new aircraft would be powered by a 700 hp Wright XR-1510-12 air-cooled radial engine, driving a three blade propeller.

BuAer approved the proposal and gave the new aircraft the designation XSBC-2, although the original BuNo 9225, was reassigned to the replacement. The XSBC-2 made its first flight on 9 December 1935, and a few months later it was re-engined with a Pratt & Whitney R-1535-82 engine since the original Wright engine had proven to be mechanically unreliable. As a result of the engine change, the prototype underwent still another designation change, this time to XSBC-3. With the new engine, BuAer awarded Curtiss a 2,045,783 dollar production contract for eighty-three aircraft under the designation SBC-3.

Development

XF12C-1

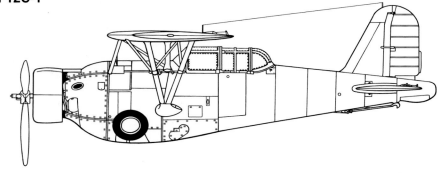

XS4C-1/XSBC-1

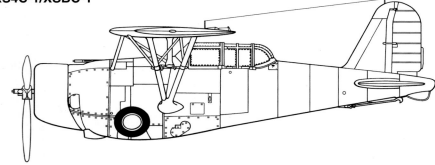

XSBC-2

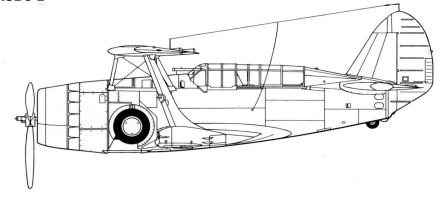

SBC-3

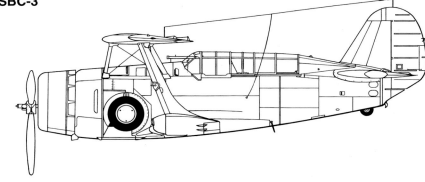

SBC-4

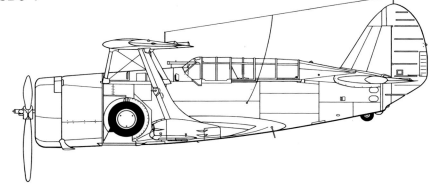

SBC-3

The SBC-3 differed very little from the prototype. Production aircraft were powered by a slightly more powerful engine, the Pratt & Whitney R-1535-94 air-cooled radial driving a three blade Hamilton Standard propeller. The two place aircraft had the crew seated under a sliding canopy with separate sliding sections for each crew member. The rear observer/gunner was equipped with a single .30 caliber machine gun, which was stowed under the folding turtle deck when not in use. The main landing gear retracted into wells in the forward fuselage, while the tail wheel semi-retracted into a well at the tail, being partially exposed when retracted. The fuselage was all metal, while the wings were metal with fabric covering, connected by I struts. The upper wing outer panels were swept back at a slight angle and included the ailerons. The lower wing included the full span flaps which were used both for landing and as dive brakes during dive-bombing operations. The pilot was provided a single .30 caliber machine gun mounted in the starboard forward fuselage. A single 500 pound bomb could be carried on the lower fuselage centerline suspended from a bomb displacement swing. For long range scouting missions, a forty-five gallon drop tank could be carried in place of the bomb.

During this time period, BuAer had only awarded production contracts for monoplane aircraft, the exception being the SBC-3. Because of this, and the acceptance of the XSBC-4 in January of 1938, the SBC design would carry on well past our entry into the Second World War with front line service on USS HORNET and with the Marine Corps on Samoa.

The early competitors of the XF12C-1, the Douglas XFD-1 and the Vought XF3U-1 were not awarded contracts by BuAer, although the Vought design was modified in February of 1934 and became the XSBU-1, which later went into production as the SBU-1 and equipped Scouting Squadron One B (VS-1B) and Scouting Squadron Forty-two (VS-42) on USS RANGER CV-4, during 1936 and 1937 respectively. Scouting Squadron Two B (VS-2B) and

The XSBC-2 biplane parked on the Curtiss ramp on 1 April 1936. The aircraft featured a Wright XR-1510-12 engine, enlarged canopy and retractable arresting hook. The aircraft was painted overall Light Gray with Black lettering. (Curtiss via Peter Bowers)

Helldiver Evolution

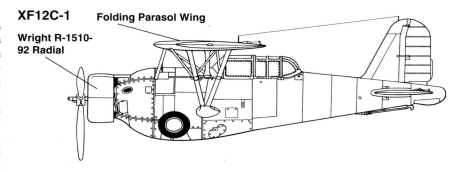

XF12C-1   Folding Parasol Wing

Wright R-1510-92 Radial

XS4C-1/XSBC-1   Fixed Parasol Wing

Curtiss SR1820F-3 Radial

Exposed Arresting Hook

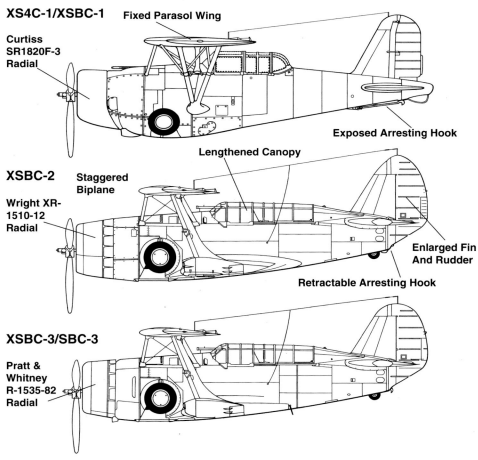

Lengthened Canopy

XSBC-2   Staggered Biplane

Wright XR-1510-12 Radial

Enlarged Fin And Rudder

Retractable Arresting Hook

XSBC-3/SBC-3

Pratt & Whitney R-1535-82 Radial

The XSBC-3 on final approach for landing at NAS Anacostia, Washington, D.C. on 10 April 1936. The aircraft featured full trailing edge flaps on the lower wing. (Navy via Peter Bowers)

The XSBC-3 also differed from the XSBC-2 in that it was fitted with a Hamilton Standard propeller in place of the Curtiss Electric propeller used on the XSBC-2. (Navy via Peter Bowers)

Scouting Squadron Three B (VS-3B) on USS LEXINGTON CV-2, also received their SBUs in 1936.

The first deliveries of the SBC-3 began on 17 July 1937. Just two weeks before, the Navy began redesignating carrier-based squadrons, giving the squadron the same number as the hull number of its assigned carrier, VS-2 on CV-2, etc.

During this time, carrier squadrons were flying the Boeing F4B-4, Grumman F2F-1 and F3F-1, Curtiss BFC-2, Vought SBU-1, Martin BM-1 and Great Lakes TG-2. It was still a biplane Navy, but changes were on the way and would be seen by the end of 1937, when the Douglas TBD-1 and Vought SB2U-1 came into squadron service.

The first Navy squadron to receive the SBC-3 was Scouting Squadron Five (VS-5) aboard USS YORKTOWN (CV-5). VS-5, at this time, was not yet carrier-based, since the YORKTOWN was still undergoing sea trials off the Virginia capes and would not take aboard any aircraft until 10 November 1937, when LCDR Clifton A.F. Sprague made the first take-off and landing in a Vought O3U-3 of the ship's Utility unit.

The first SBC-3s came aboard on 10 December 1937, when VS-5 together with VF-5 (F2F-1s) were hoisted aboard at pier 7 of the Norfolk Naval Base. Aboard USS SARATOGA (CV-3), VS-3 had received its first SBC-3s and they were soon carrier qualified. By November of 1937, VS-3 had a total of fourteen of the new scout-bombers on their inventory.

Scouting Squadron Six (VS-6) began receiving the SBC-3 while their carrier, USS ENTERPRISE (CV-6) was not yet in commission. By November of 1937, VS-6 had eighteen SBC-3s and by the time they went aboard ENTERPRISE, they had increased this number to twenty. From May of 1938, until they were replaced by Douglas SBD-2 Dauntless dive-bombers in early 1941, VS-6 maintained at least seventeen SBC-3s on hand. While waiting for their carrier to be commissioned, VS-6 operated, from time to time, aboard USS YORKTOWN, gaining valuable carrier time.

The seventy-sixth production SBC-3 was chosen to undergo further development into what was hoped would become an improved version of the SBC-3. The aircraft was re-engined with a 950 hp Wright R-1820-22 single row, air-cooled, radial under the designation XSBC-4.

The SBC-3s of VS-5 and VS-6 figured prominently in Fleet Problem XX, a war game which took place in January of 1939. The YORKTOWN, ENTERPRISE and LEXINGTON were assigned to the White Fleet, while RANGER was the sole carrier assigned to the Black Fleet. The two forces were fighting to gain control over "Green" which represented a revolution plagued nation.

YORKTOWN's SBC-3s, with assistance from Torpedo Squadron Five's (VT-5) TBD-1s, attacked USS NORTHHAMPTON (CA-26) and successfully put the big cruiser out of action. The umpires ruled that NORTHHAMPTON's guns had "shot down" two of the SBC-3s of VS-5 during the attack.

During the exercise, the RANGER Air Group attacked the ENTERPRISE and put the new carrier out of action. Attacks were made on principal targets by the SBC-3s of VS-5 including an attack on a Black battleship in which all seventeen of the squadron's aircraft participated. Five of the dive bombers were "lost" on this mission. Shortly after this engagement, the White force was declared the winner. The pilots of VS-5 and 6 had proven themselves and their biplane dive-bombers.

The SBC-3 toiled on through the late 1930s and early 1940s. Some of the -3s were assigned to fighting squadrons and used as utility aircraft, towing target sleeves, transporting personnel, etc. Fighting Squadron Three (VF-3) aboard SARATOGA, Fighting Six on ENTERPRISE and YORKTOWN's Fighting Five all had a SBC-3 utility aircraft. Fighting Squadron Four (VF-4) on RANGER soon followed suit during 1940. The SBCs fit right in with the VF squadrons and presented no special maintenance problems.

Carrier Air Group commanders (CAGs) on the SARATOGA, ENTERPRISE, YORKTOWN and RANGER flew SBC-3s at various times in the pre-war Navy. The Vought SB2U also was used in this role in this same time period. The aircraft type chosen by the CAG varied according to personal preference and aircraft availability. Later, when the SBC-4 became

The front cockpit of a SBC-3 Helldiver. The circular object above the instrument panel was the telescopic gun sight. The rudder peddles were located just below the instrument panel. (National Archives via R.J. Cressman)

The rear cockpit (looking forward) reveals the radio panel, socket for a control stick and rudder peddles. In an emergency, the gunner could fly the aircraft from the rear cockpit. (National Archives via R.J. Cressman)

available, the ENTERPRISE CAG adopted BuNo 1295 for his personal use.

The only SBC-3 assigned to the Marine Corps went to Marine Fighting Squadron Two (VMF-2) in San Diego, California during 1938. This SBC-3 (BuNo 0521) operated as 2-MF-19 until sent to the Battle Fleet Pool in June of 1939.

When the SBC-3 entered service with the Navy and up until our entry into the Second World War, carrier aircraft were equipped with flotation bags which deployed automatically in the event of a forced landing in water. This was supposed to save the aircraft if the impact

9

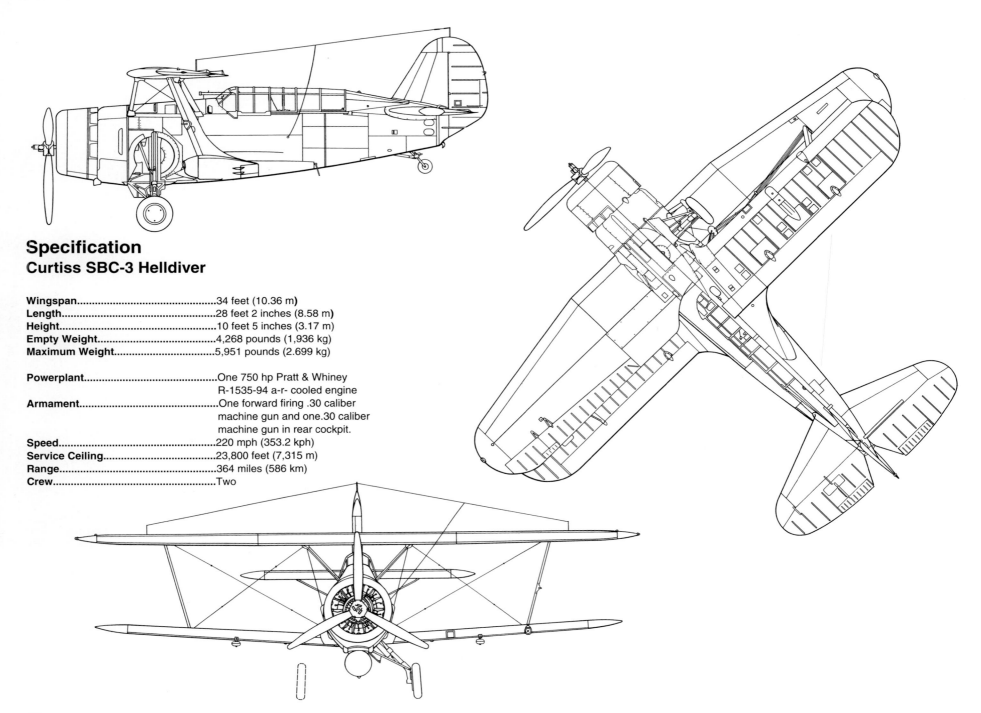

Specification
Curtiss SBC-3 Helldiver

Wingspan	34 feet (10.36 m)
Length	28 feet 2 inches (8.58 m)
Height	10 feet 5 inches (3.17 m)
Empty Weight	4,268 pounds (1,936 kg)
Maximum Weight	5,951 pounds (2.699 kg)
Powerplant	One 750 hp Pratt & Whiney R-1535-94 a-r- cooled engine
Armament	One forward firing .30 caliber machine gun and one.30 caliber machine gun in rear cockpit.
Speed	220 mph (353.2 kph)
Service Ceiling	23,800 feet (7,315 m)
Range	364 miles (586 km)
Crew	Two

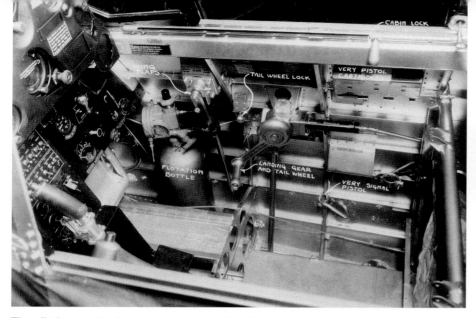

The pilot's seat has been removed from this SBC-3 cockpit. The right cockpit sidewall contained the landing gear retraction crank, tail wheel lock and wing flap controls. (National Archives via R. J. Cressman)

This is the fixed .30 caliber machine gun installation on a SBC-3. The gun was installed in the starboard side of the fuselage. The bar coming back off the gun to the cockpit was the charging handle, which was operated by the pilot to chamber the first round into the gun before firing. (National Archives via R. J. Cressman)

The first production SBC-3 (BuNo 0507) on the ramp at the Naval Aircraft Factory on 10 December 1937. This Helldiver was stricken from the inventory on 30 June 1938, after being damaged beyond repair during static testing. (Navy via Peter Bowers)

was not too severe. From time to time these bags deployed while in flight, causing no end of grief for the crew. The SBC-3 did not escape at least one such episode and it happened to a pilot and observer in VS-6.

At 0730 on 30 October 1940, Ensign M.J. Rozamus, A-V (N), USNR, took off from Naval Air Station Ford Island, Pearl Harbor, Hawaii in his SBC-3 (BuNo 0517) accompanied by his observer, RM-3/c Evon Gambrell. The VS-6 pilot was headed for some Individual Battle Practice (IBP) bombing, at Kaena Point.

Upon recovery from his second dive, Ensign Rozamus closed his dive flaps, opened the engine cowl flaps and turned the pre-heat on full cold. When he looked at his port and starboard wings, he noticed that the port wing's floatation bag and wires were visible. It appeared as though the bag was protruding a few inches out of its stowage compartment. The panel normally covering the compartment was also missing. He then told his observer, Radioman Gambrell, to visually check the bag as well. Gambrell said he could see the bag.

Ensign Rozamus then called 6-S-10 and requested permission to return to Ford Island. He also called 6-S-7 to accompany him. He saw 6-S-7 pass underneath his aircraft going in the opposite direction. Suddenly, the SBC-3 lurched into a slow roll to the left. It was now apparent that the floatation bag had deployed. He applied full force on the stick to the right, put the propeller into positive low and advanced the throttle until 34" of manifold pressure was indicated. The SBC-3 continued to turn to the left, so he told his observer to be ready to jump. He felt Garmbrell insert the stick into it's receptacle in the rear cockpit and although they both applied full right stick, the aircraft continued its roll to the left.

He was now inverted so Ensign Rozarnus told his radioman to jump. He felt him relax on the stick, so Rozaraus then reached for his safety belt. He jerked the belt buckle and let go of the stick, dropping out of the cockpit. He fell a few hundred feet, pulled the rip cord and saw his radioman's parachute below him and to the south. Approximately fifty minutes later a PBY-1 from Patrol Squadron Twenty-Four (VP-24), 24-P-8, picked him up. A PBY-2 from Patrol Squadron Twenty-Five (VP-25), 25-P-7, picked up his observer, Radioman Gambrell. Nether man was injured in the incident.

This SBC-3 Helldiver (BuNo 0527) was flown by the Air Group Commander of USS YORK-TOWN during 1940. The diagonal fuselage stripe and tail were in Red, the color assigned to all squadron aircraft attached to USS YORKTOWN (CV-5) at the time. (D. F. Kauer via W. T. Larkins)

5-S-1 was flown by the commanding officer of Scouting Squadron Five. The fuselage stripe, cowling and tail were in Red. This SBC-3 went on to serve with VS-5, VF-4 and VS-6. It was lost at sea on 24 August 1941, while serving as a trainer out of NAS Norfolk, Virginia. (D. W. Lucabaugh Collection)

This was the third aircraft of the 1st section of VS-5 aboard USS YORKTOWN (CV-5) during 1940. The lower portion of the cowling and tail were in Red. (W. T. Larkins)

Eventually time caught up to the SBC-3 and the classy biplane began to take on more of a support role within Naval Aviation. By 7 December 1941, the SBC-3 was mainly being used as a trainer at NAS Miami, Florida. The Douglas SBD was now serving on our carriers in the VB and VS role.

A number of SBC-3s remained in service through to the mid-point of the Second World War. The last twenty-five aircraft were stricken from the list during 1944. The longest to survive were twelve SBC-3s based at NAS Jacksonville, Florida which were used as advanced trainers. They stayed on until 31 October 1944.

The second aircraft of the 2nd section of VS-5 aboard YORKTOWN during 1940. The upper portion of the cowling was in White. 5-S-5 later served with VS-6 and as the personal aircraft of the Air Group Commander aboard USS ENTERPRISE (CV-6). It was stricken from the inventory on 6 December 1941 at Naval Air Station, Miami, Florida. (W. T. Larkins)

This aircraft was flown by the 3rd section leader of VS-5. 5-S-7 carries the Man-of-War squadron insignia of VS-5 on the fuselage side under the cockpit. The tail is Red, the cowling and fuselage stripe are True Blue, while the S and dashes are in White. (H. Nolen via W. T. Larkins)

(Lower Right) This SBC-3 on the ramp at the Curtiss factory on 29 September 1937, was painted in the markings of the leader of section 4 of VS-5 at the factory. The fuselage band and cowling were in Black. The aircraft remained in service until 31 October 1944, when it was stricken from the inventory at NAS Jacksonville, Florida. (Curtiss via D. W. Lucabaugh)

It appears that 5-S-12 is being flown solo without a rear gunner/radio operator. The aircraft had a Red tail. The SBC-3 served with VS-5 from 15 October 1937 to 30 August 1939. It also served with VS-6 and VS-3 before being retired. (Navy via W. L. Swisher)

A pair of two SBC-3s on the ramp at the Union Air Terminal, Burbank, California during June of 1939. Both aircraft carry the Man-of-War insignia on the fuselage. The Bird was Black with a Red throat, the diamond was White with a Red outline. (W. L. Swisher)

The leader of section six after a wheels up landing on 22 September 1938. The pilot was thrown from the aircraft during a high speed dive. The rear seat gunner, realizing the pilot was gone, managed to land the aircraft near the airfield at NAS Cape May, New Jersey. He received a Navy commendation for landing the aircraft safely. The fuselage band and cowling were Lemon Yellow. (Navy via D.W. Lucahaugh)

A formation of SBC-3s of VS-3 fly a tight formation during 1939. The aircraft carry Lemon Yellow tails, indicating that they were serving aboard USS LEXINGTON (CV-2). (Navy via J. H. Weathers, Jr.)

Nine SBC-3s of Scouting Squadron Three (VS-3) fly a close formation over the mountains. The tail color was White, the assigned color of USS SARATOGA (CV-3). The first SBC-3 to arrive on SARATOGA came aboard on 2 October 1937. (Navy via B. Donato)

This SBC-3 (BuNo 0571) was flown by the squadron commander of VS-3 during 1939. The aircraft has the Red cowling and fuselage stripe of the squadron CO but lacks the Red chevron marking normally carried on top of the wing center section. The turtleback is folded down so that the gunner could deploy his weapon. This Helldiver later served with VS-5 and VS-6. (Navy via H. Gann)

This is aircraft number 2 of section one of VS-3 during 1938. The top of the cowling was Red and the "Pointer Dog" squadron insignia was carried on the fuselage side below the pilot's cockpit. This aircraft was lost at sea on 29 August 1939, while serving with VS-5. Originally delivered on 29 August 1937, it had logged a total of 381.7 flight hours before its loss. (W.T. Larkins)

(Right and Above Right) These SBC-3s of VS-3 collided on take-off from Naval Air Station, North Island, San Diego, California on 7 September 1938. Both aircraft 3-S-2 (BuNo 0511) and 3-S-5 (BuNo 0569) were later repaired and flew again. (Navy via D.W. Lucabaugh)

A SBC-3 Helldiver (BuNo 0512) of VS-3 running up its engine prior to take off during 1937. The aircraft carries a White E on the forward fuselage, awarded for excellence in gunnery. This Helldiver later served with Bombing Squadron Four (VB-4) aboard USS RANGER (CV-4) during late 1940. (W. T. Larkins)

Three-Sail-Four (3-S-4) on the ramp at NAS Oakland, California during 1940. The aircraft had a White tail, fuselage band and cowling. The "Pointer Dog" insignia was carried just forward of the aircraft side numbers. It later served with VS-201 aboard USS LONG ISLAND (AVG-1) and ended its days at NAS Jacksonville, Florida on 31 October 1944. (W. T. Larkins)

These aircraft both carry the same fuselage code (3-S-7), but have different BuNos. BuNo 0516 (below) made a wheels up landing at NAS North Island, San Diego on 2 November 1937, while BuNo 0554 (above) ground looped after a night instrument landing again at NAS North Island on 20 November 1939. (Navy via D.W. Lucabaugh)

This SBC-3, Three-Sail-Five of VS-3, rests on its upper wing after turning over on landing. The damage was limited to the upper wing and vertical fin. The aircraft has a bomb rack installed on the lower wing undersurface. (Navy via D. W. Lucabaugh)

This SBC-3 (BuNo 0541) of Scouting Squadron Three (VS-3) made a wheels up landing on 4 November 1937. The aircraft had the lower portion of the cowling painted Lemon Yellow. The bent back propeller blades indicate that the engine was still running when the aircraft went onto her belly. (Navy vla D. W. Lucabaugh)

When VS-3 went aboard USS LEXINGTON during 1939 for the ship's Caribbean tour, they repainted the tails of their aircraft Lemon Yellow. This aircraft was flown by Ensign L. E. Kinnan and carried a Bombing E on the forward fuselage and a communications C award on the rear fuselage near the fuselage number 17. (Peter Bowers)

Lieutenant Commander T. S. Combs flies 6-S-1 (BuNo 0565) during a fly-by on the commissioning day of USS ENTERPRISE (CV-6, 12 May 1938). The other two aircraft are an F3F-2 of Fighting Six, flown by Lieutenant H. L. Jennings and a TBD-1 of Torpedo Six TBD-1 flown by LCDR D. P. Johnson. (Navy/National Archives)

SBC-3s of Scouting Six (VS-6) on the flight line at NAS Norfolk, Virginia. At this time the squadron was based aboard USS ENTERPRISE (CV-6). (Navy via D.W. Lucabaugh)

This VS-6 SBC-3 (BuNo 0565) had a True Blue tail. The fuselage stripe, engine cowling and wing chevron were in Red. (National Archives via R. J. Cressman)

A SBC-3, flown by the ENTERPRISE Air Group Commander, prepares to launch from the flight deck of USS YORKTOWN during carrier qualifications on the Southern Drill Grounds. The billboard behind the aircraft, giving the ships course and speed, was unique to the YORKTOWN and ENTERPRISE. (National Archives via R. J. Cressman)

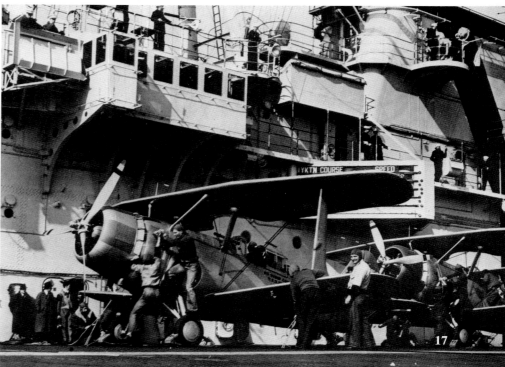

17

A SBC-3 (BuNo 0569) makes a low pass down the starboard side of USS MUSTIN (DD-413) on 26 May 1940. The upper portion of the engine cowling was in White. (National Archives via R. J. Cressman)

A SBC-3 of VS-6 is hoisted for transportation back to the squadron maintenance hangar after it damaged the landing gear during a ground loop at NAS Norfolk on 5 December 1940. (Navy via D.W. Lucabaugh)

Six-Sail-Nine sits on its belly waiting to be lifted back on its wheels after a wheels up landing at NAS Norfolk, Virginia on 22 March 1938. The Aztec Indian insignia of VS-6 is visible on the fuselage side under the cockpit. (Navy via D. W. Lucabaugh)

This SBC-3 (BuNo 0225) was used by Fighting Six as a utility aircraft during 1937. It often flew as a lead navigation aircraft on cross-country flights. (W. T. Larkins)

This SBC was at NAS Oakland, California during August of 1941. The aircraft carried unusual markings that did not identity its assigned unit. (Peter Bowers)

The Marine Corps had only one SBC-3 (BuNo 0521). It was assigned to Marine Fighter Squadron Two (VMF-2) at NAS North Island, San Diego, California. It was delivered on 14 September 1937 and remained active until 17 July 1939. The tail stripes are (front to back) Blue/White/Red and the aircraft carried the Marine globe and anchor insignia on the fuselage side and the squadron insignia on the fin. The crew chief was M/SGT E. Devendorph. (W.T. Larkins)

This SBC-3 was assigned to Fighter Squadron Five (VF-5) before being transferred to Naval Air Station Miami, Florida for use as an advanced trainer. The aircraft suffered a landing gear failure on 12 April 1942, but was repaired and put back in service. It continued in use until 30 October 1943 when it was retired. (Navy via D. W. Lucabaugh)

This SBC-3 was towed back to its home base after the engine seized on a cross-country flight. The propeller was removed and a PBY-5A served as the tow aircraft. The aircraft was camouflaged in Non-specular Blue Gray over Light Gray. The national insignia indicates that the incident took place between mid-May of 1942 and June of 1943. (Navy/National Archives)

This PBY-5A Catalina served as the tow aircraft. The trip was from Akron, Ohio back to Naval Air Station Anacostia, Washington D.C. The Catalina was also camouflaged in Non-specular Blue Gray over Light Gray. (Navy/National Archives)

SBC-4

The Curtiss XSBC-4 started out as the seventy-sixth production SBC-3. Curtiss began the modification to the basic airframe in February of 1938. The biggest change was the installation of a more powerful and larger diameter 950 hp Wright R-1820-22 air-cooled radial. The new engine led to a modification of the cowling and forward fuselage to accommodate the larger diameter of the Curtiss power plant. With the more powerful engine, the aircraft was able to carry a larger bomb load, up to 1,000 pounds, on the centerline bomb rack. The forward firing armament was also changed from a single .30 caliber machine gun to a single .50 caliber machine gun.

The aircraft was accepted by the Navy almost immediately. BuAer issued a contract for fifty-eight aircraft under the designation SBC-4 (BuNos 1268-1325) on 5 January 1938. On 27 July a second contract was issued for another thirty-one (BuNos 1474-1504). This was followed on 13 August by a third contract for thirty-five additional aircraft (BuNos 1809-1843).

In a move designed to upgrade the aircraft being flown by Scouting Squadron Two (VS-2) on USS LEXINGTON, it was decided that they would be the first unit to take delivery of the new SBC-4. Scouting Two had been flying the Vought SBU-1 since late-1935 when they were designated VS-3B and equipped with a combination of Grumman SF-1s and Vought SBUs.

The first SBC-4 off the production line went to NAS Anacostia, outside Washington, D.C. where it was put through a series of tests and an experimental program.

The XSBC-4 started out as the seventy-sixth production SBC-3 (BuNo 0582). It was re-engined with a larger diameter 950 hp Wright R-1820-22 radial with a modified cowling. The aircraft served with VMF-1, VMJ-1 and Air Base Detachment One, Quantico, Virginia before being sent to Alaska. (Navy via Peter Bowers)

The XSBC-4 was sent to NAS Sitka, Alaska where it served as an anti-submarine patrol aircraft until August of 1944. It made seventeen ASW patrols but did not sight or sink any enemy submarines. (Peter Bowers)

In March of 1939, LCDR James B. Taylor, Jr., USNR, one of the top Navy test pilots, volunteered to test the SBC-4 (BuNo 1268) in a series of high speed dives at Dahlgren, Maryland. At one point in the decent the SBC-4 went out of control, although Taylor managed to recover. The maneuver was violent enough to tear the practice bomb and bomb rack from the aircraft, while the over-stress permanently deformed the wing. The stress encountered in the pull-out deceleration had proved more severe than the aircraft structure had been designed to withstand.

Observers considered Taylor's achievement as a "voluntary act in the face of great danger, well above normal expectations." Unfortunately, LCDR Taylor's test flying came to an fatal end in the crash of the XF4F-6 on 25 May 1942.

The number two production SBC-4 was chosen to be displayed at the 1939 New York Worlds Fair in the Hall Of Aviation. This -4 arrived at the Fair on 29 May 1939 and by October of 1940, it was flying with VS-2 as 2-S-13.

By 26 June 1939, VS-2 was fully equipped with SBC-4s. Scouting Two was led, at this time, by LCDR John Warburton King. King was very well liked by his squadron and respected by all hands. He knew war was coming and set about making VS-2 as prepared as possible for that event. He put the squadron on a tough schedule of night flying and dive bombing. There were many flights from San Diego to Phoenix, Arizona, under cover of darkness. The squadron carrier qualified at night and flew night missions against the target ship USS UTAH, AG-16 (ex-BB-31) at night. They would search out the ship as she steamed somewhere off the California coast and once the squadron located the UTAH, two pilots (previously designated as illuminators) would drop parachute flares and continued to do so while the rest of the squadron made their runs on the old target ship. Diving into an illuminated area, then pulling up into complete darkness was pretty exciting for the pilots, and to quote a former VS-2 pilot, CAPT Charles E. Roemer USN, Ret. (then an Ensign) "Why there were not casualties out of that, I'll never understand." John King continued putting VS-2 and their SBC-4s through a rigorous and exacting training schedule. One time, on a cross country flight he took the entire squadron of eighteen SBC-4s, in formation, down inside the Grand Canyon below the rim.

Fuselage Development

SBC-3

Pratt & Whitney R-1535-82 Radial

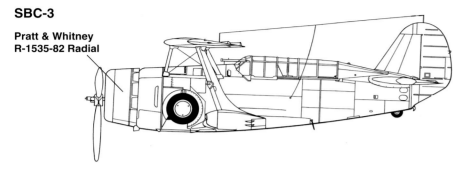

SBC-4

950 hp Wright R-1820-22 Radial Engine

Larger Diameter Cowling and Revised Underfuselage Contour

During a deployment to the Hawaiian Islands, he took the squadron down inside the Kilauea Crater during an eruption

Many in the squadron felt that the intensive training they took part in resulted in a number of wartime and postwar leaders that came from the squadron. As far as the SBC-4, VS-2 found it to be a pilot's dream to fly. It was extremely reliable and lived up to most of the claims made for it.

The Marine Corps received one SBC-4 from the first batch of production aircraft which was delivered during 1939. BuNo 1287 went to VMF-2 on 7 July 1939.

At that same time, one SBC-4 each went to the Commander Aircraft Scouting Force and the Commanding General Fleet Marine Force. They were BuNos 1289 and 1290 respectively. BuNo 1290 eventually was ordered to Peru in October of 1940 where it served with the United States Naval Aviation Mission to Peru, at Lima. The aircraft survived until 28 February 1943, when it was stricken from the inventory.

Because of the expanding aviation program within the Naval Air Reserve, the SBC-4s coming off the Curtiss production line were sent directly to Naval Reserve Air Bases throughout the United States. The decision to equip the Reserves with the SBC-4 was made by the Chief of the Bureau of Aeronautics, Rear Admiral A. B. Cook, as early as September of 1938.

The first SBC-4s delivered to the reserves was BuNo 1475 which was delivered to the Naval Reserve Air Base (NRAB) at Chicago, Illinois on 17 June 1939. It was followed by a second aircraft BuNo 1476 the same day. By September of 1939, when the Second World War began

in Europe, Chicago's VS-9R would show six SBC-4s on board the station. By years-end, a total of fifty-seven SBC-4s had been delivered to the following NRABs: Kansas City, Missouri (Fairfax Airport), Minneapolis, Minnesota, Detroit, Michigan (Grosse Ile), St. Louis, Missouri (Robertson), Chicago, Illinois (Glenview), Long Beach, California, Seattle Washington, and Oakland, California

The SBC-4 became the mainstay of Naval Reserve Aviation in the years immediately preceding our entry into the Second World War. The Reserve bases provided equipment and facilities for the periodic training of Marine Corps and Naval Reserve pilots so that they could keep their flight proficiency up to par with their counterparts in the Fleet, should they be called up in the event of a national emergency. The bases also served as training sites for giving selected seamen applicants elimination flight training prior to their being appointed as aviation cadets. The Elimination Base students received four to six weeks training at these "E" bases where they were paid $33.00 a month plus a dollar a day subsistence allowance. They mainly flew the Naval Aircraft Factory N3N-1 or N3N-3 "Yellow Peril" biplane trainer and were rated as Seamen, Second Class, V-5 (Aviation), USNR.

Events in Europe were soon to have an impact on U. S. Naval Aviation. A situation soon developed that started with good intentions, but ended with the destruction of a number of SBC-4s.

Scouting Squadron Two (VS-2) lined-up for inspection on the ramp at Naval Air Station North Island, San Diego, California during 1939. Scouting Two was the first squadron to fully re-equip with the SBC-4 and was based aboard the carrier USS LEXINGTON (CV-2). The unit's tail color was Lemon Yellow. (Navy via CAPT C. E. Roemer USN, Ret.)

A SBC-4 (BuNo 1288), 2-S-1 of VS-2 in flight over the Pacific during 1939. The reverse placement of the Red wing chevron was unique to VS-2. The tail was Lemon Yellow and the fuselage stripe and cowling were in Red. (Navy via Jansson/Lucabaugh)

(Above) This SBC-4 (BuNo 1277), Two-Sail-Nine of VS-2, was flown by Ensign Charles E. Roemer during 1939. The aircraft was the third aircraft in the third section. The aircraft's plane captain, AMM3 Lierman is in the front cockpit, while the radioman/gunner, RM2 Congdon is in the rear cockpit. The plane captain was responsible for the day-to-day maintenance of the aircraft and for ensuring that it was ready for flight. (CAPT C. E. Roemer, USN, Ret.)

(Left) This SBC-4 (BuNo 1295) on the ramp at Naval Air Station Oakland, California during 1940, was the personal aircraft of the Air Group Commander, USS ENTERPRISE air group. The aircraft carried a True Blue tail, fuselage stripe and cowling stripes. The USS ENTERPRISE insignia, a Blue sailing ship on a White circle with the legend ENT below it in Blue, was carried on both sides of the lower rear fuselage. The aircraft has been fitted with an external fuel tank on the centerline bomb rack. (Peter Bowers)

Cowling Development

SBC-3 Pratt & Whitney R-1535-82 Radial

SBC-4 Wright R-1820-22 Radial

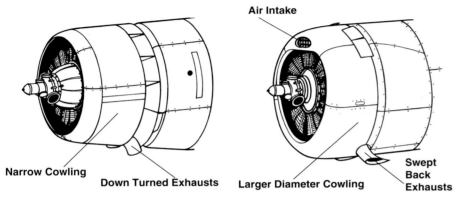

Air Intake

Narrow Cowling

Down Turned Exhausts

Larger Diameter Cowling

Swept Back Exhausts

On 8 September 1940, Secretary of the Navy, Frank Knox, took-off from the USS ENTERPRISE on a VIP flight. The Secretary flew in the Air Group Commander's aircraft which had True Blue striping around the cowling. The triangle on top of the wing was also in True Blue. (Navy via D. W. Lucabaugh)

LCDR Edward C. Ewen was the pilot that flew Secretary of the Navy Knox off ENTERPRISE on 8 September 1940. The "Big E" was steaming off Oahu, Hawaii at the time and the Secretary was departing for meetings at Pearl Harbor. (National Archives via R. J. Cressman)

(Below) A deck crewman lies under the wing of a SBC-4 on USS ENTERPRISE. His job was to remove the wheel chocks before the aircraft began its take-off roll. The aircraft has a bomb rack mounted under the outboard wing panel. (National Archives via R. J. Cressman)

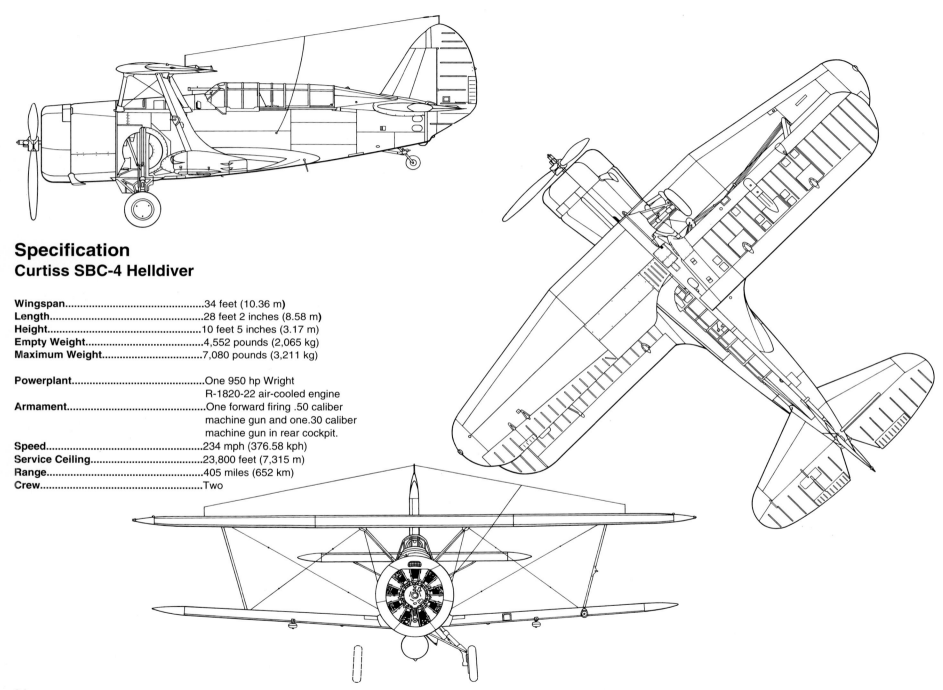

Specification
Curtiss SBC-4 Helldiver

Wingspan..34 feet (10.36 m**)**
Length..28 feet 2 inches (8.58 m**)**
Height..10 feet 5 inches (3.17 m)
Empty Weight..4,552 pounds (2,065 kg)
Maximum Weight....................................7,080 pounds (3,211 kg)

Powerplant..One 950 hp Wright
 R-1820-22 air-cooled engine
Armament..One forward firing .50 caliber
 machine gun and one.30 caliber
 machine gun in rear cockpit.
Speed..234 mph (376.58 kph)
Service Ceiling....................................23,800 feet (7,315 m)
Range..405 miles (652 km)
Crew..Two

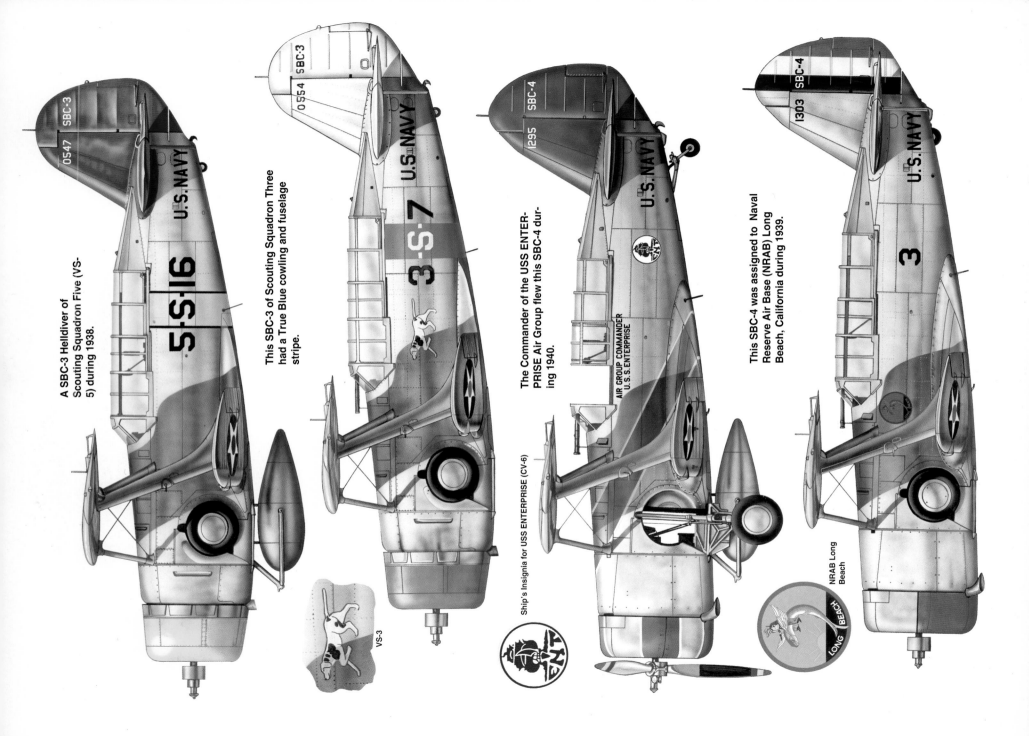

A SBC-3 Helldiver of Scouting Squadron Five (VS-5) during 1938.

This SBC-3 of Scouting Squadron Three had a True Blue cowling and fuselage stripe.

VS-3

Ship's Insignia for USS ENTERPRISE (CV-6)

The Commander of the USS ENTERPRISE Air Group flew this SBC-4 during 1940.

AIR GROUP COMMANDER
U.S.S. ENTERPRISE

This SBC-4 was assigned to Naval Reserve Air Base (NRAB) Long Beach, California during 1939.

NRAB Long Beach

LONG BEACH

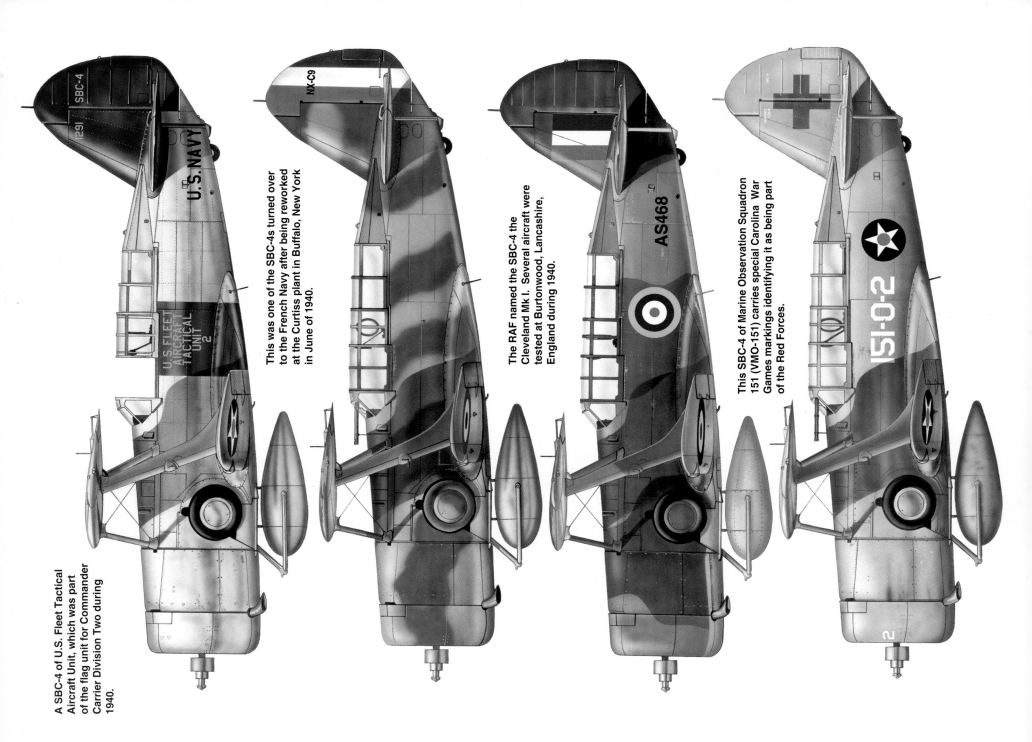

A SBC-4 of U.S. Fleet Tactical Aircraft Unit, which was part of the flag unit for Commander Carrier Division Two during 1940.

This was one of the SBC-4s turned over to the French Navy after being reworked at the Curtiss plant in Buffalo, New York in June of 1940.

The RAF named the SBC-4 the Cleveland Mk I. Several aircraft were tested at Burtonwood, Lancashire, England during 1940.

This SBC-4 of Marine Observation Squadron 151 (VMO-151) carries special Carolina War Games markings identifying it as being part of the Red Forces.

A SBC-4 Helldiver (BuNo 1322) of the Naval Reserve Air Base, Anacostia, Washington D.C. on the grass at Logan Field, Baltimore, Maryland during 1940. The fuselage stripe and cowling were Red while the tail was True Blue. (B. Ederr via D. W. Lucabaugh)

A SBC-4 begins its take-off roll from USS ENTERPRISE during 1940. The aircraft had a True Blue triangle on top of the wing instead of the more usual wing chevron. (Navy via D.W. Lucabaugh)

SBC-4s on the line at the Naval Reserve Air Base (NRAB) Chicago, Illinois during 1939. The SBC in the foreground was later passed to the French Navy during June of 1940. (Navy via C. L. Jansson)

A NRAB Seattle, Washington SBC-4 on the ramp at Boeing Field, Seattle. The aircraft ended its service life with VMSB-151. After being retired it served as an instructional airframe with a training unit at Norman, Oklahoma until 8 October 1943, when it was finally stricken from the inventory. (Peter Bowers)

This factory fresh SBC-4 on the ramp at the Curtiss facility on 27 July 1939, was painted with a Willow Green tail for delivery to Naval Reserve Air Base Seattle, Washington. The aircraft (BuNo 1502) was later destroyed in a crash at NAS Corpus Christi, Texas on 2 May 1942. (Curtiss via D. W. Lucabaugh)

A SBC-4 of the Golden Gaters (Naval Reserve Air Base, Oakland, California) on the Curtiss factory ramp on 1 August 1939. SBC-4s coming off the assembly line were often painted at the factory in the markings of the unit that was to receive the aircraft. (Curtiss via Peter Bowers)

A SBC-4 (BuNo 1302) from NRAB Long Beach, California on the ramp at Grand Central Air Terminal, Glendale, California during 1940. The top half of the cowling was Red, while the tail stripes were (front to back) Blue, White, Red. This aircraft went on to serve with Marine Observation Squadron 151. (Peter Bowers)

A SBC-4 of the Oakland Naval Reserve Air Base makes practice touch-and-go landings with everything down but the tail hook during 1940. The fuselage stripe and cowling are in Red. (W. T. Larkins)

28

A SBC-4 (BuNo 1819) of NRAB Kansas City, Missouri prepares to taxi out for another training mission. The aircraft had a White cowling and tail. (C.W. Phillips via W.T. Larkins)

A SBC-4 (BuNo 1303) of NRAB Long Beach, California prepares for take-off on Navy Day, 1939. The base insignia was carried on the fuselage side below the windscreen. In April of 1939, Curtiss proposed a new Helldiver variant, the XSBC-5, which would have been powered by a R-1820-34 driving a ten foot three inch propeller, with larger wheels. The Navy felt that the biplane had reached the end of its useful development and the project was abandoned. (D.W. Lucabaugh Collection)

This SBC-4 (BuNo 1318) of NRAB Kansas City made a wheels up landing in a field near NAS Miami, Florida on 27 January 1941. The fuselage stripe and cowling were Lemon Yellow and the tail was Willow Green. (Navy via D.W. Lucabaugh)

The SBC-4 had full length trailing edge flaps on the lower wing. This SBC-4 (BuNo 1305) was assigned to NRAB New York at Floyd Bennett Field during 1940. (H. Levy via Peter Bowers)

This SBC-4 (BuNo 1816) at NRAB Oakland had a Black cowling and fuselage stripe. The aircraft had the Golden Gaters squadron insignia on the fuselage side just under the windshield. (Peter Bowers)

In December of 1940, the Naval Air Reserve changed their markings, eliminating the colored cowlings and fuselage striping. The aircraft was overall Aluminum dope with Black lettering and Blue/White/Red rudder striping. (Peter Bowers)

A SBC-4 (BuNo 1813) of NRAB New York, New York. The aircraft had a True Blue tail and Red fuselage stripe and cowling. It was later delivered to the French. (R. Arnold via D. Steinbacher)

A SBC-4 at Logan Field, Baltimore, Maryland during November of 1940. The aircraft was assigned to NRAB New York. (B. Ederr via D.W. Lucabaugh)

31

A SBC-4 (BuNo 1501) of Scouting Sixteen R (VS-16R)/Marine Scouting Nine R (VMS-9R) runs up on the ramp at the Naval Reserve Air Base (NRAB) Seattle, Washington during 1940. The aircraft had a Red cowling and fuselage stripe with a WIllow Green tail. (Peter Bowers)

NRAB Oakland's SBC-4 Number 5 comes in for a landing with everything down but the arresting hook (it did not have one). The turtledeck behind the rear cockpit has been folded down. (W.T. Larkins)

Navy mechanics change the engine on a SBC-4 at NAS Norfolk, Virginia during 1941. Aboard ship it took approximately 140 man hours to change the engine, since only three men at a time could actually work on the project. (Navy)

A SBC-4 (BuNo 1269) on display at the New York Worlds Fair of 1939. The aircraft had non-standard fairings over the exhaust stubs. The aircraft later served with VS-2 where it carried the side code 2-S-12 during October of 1940. (H. Clark via D.W. Lucabaugh)

This SBC-4 served as a command transport with the First Marine Air Wing during 1940. This Helldiver remained with the Marines throughout its entire service career. (Peter Bowers)

The French Connection

By mid-1940, the situation in France had deteriorated to such a point that the nation would fall to the Germans at any time. Earlier, during 1939, the Aeronavale had ordered ninety Curtiss Model 77s, the export variant of the SBC-4. The Model 77 was the same as a SBC-4 with minor modifications to meet French requirements. The .50 caliber machine guns were replaced by Darne 7.7MM machine guns and space was provided for the French Type B parachute. Production of these aircraft was progressing slowly, since production of the Curtiss Hawk 75 and Hawk 81 fighters had priority at the Curtiss factory. Near the end of May 1940, acting on an urgent request from the French government, the White House authorized the release of fifty U.S. Navy SBC-4s of the Naval Reserve. In turn, the Navy would replace the SBC-4s with aircraft from the original French contract as they became available.

So the orders were issued on 6 June 1940, to remove the fifty SBC-4s from the various NARBs around the country and ferry them to Buffalo, New York. Not only were fifty SBCs being sent to France, but so were ten spare R-1820-34 engines, twelve spare propellers and other structural spare parts.

The aircraft were transferred from the Navy to the War Department and their journeys began. The following aircraft were selected for transfer: BuNos 1309,1310,1311, 1500, 1838, 1839, 1840 and 1841 from NRAB Anacostia, Washington, D.C. BuNos 1813, 1825,1826, 1827, 1814, 1815, 1835, 1836 and 1837 from NRAB Brooklyn, New York. BuNos 1308, 1474, 1475, 1476, 1489, 1490 and 1491 from NRAB Glenview, Illinois. BuNos 1307, 1486 and 1487 from NRAB St. Louis, Missouri. BuNos 1477, 1479, 1492, 1493, 1494, 1828 and 1503 from NRAB Kansas City. Missouri. BuNos 1480, 1481, 1482, 1495, 1820 and 1821 out of NRAB Minneapolis, Minnesota. Aircraft BuNos 1483, 1484, 1485, 1832, 1833,1834 and

This SBC-4 was overhauled and repainted in French markings at the Curtiss plant in Buffalo, New York during June of 1940. The NX-C-27 was a temporary civil registration applied for delivery to the French and all the aircraft carried the NX-C code. (E. Deigan via Peter Bowers)

A section of three ex-NRAB SBC-4s prepare for take-off from the Curtiss factory in Buffalo for delivery to the French during June of 1940. (H. Levy via Peter Bowers)

1496 from NRAB Grosse Ile, Michigan. BuNos 1810,1811 and 1822 came from NRAB Squantum, Massachusetts. Of the fifty, nineteen had less than fifty hours of flight time on the airframe and engine. At the date of transfer, one had only 7.7 hours and twenty-seven had less that 100 hours of flight time.

All of the SBC-4s that had been earmarked for France were to proceed at once to the Curtiss factory in Buffalo, New York. Once at Curtiss, the SBC-4s were immediately prepared for shipment to the French. The Darne machine guns were installed in place of our Brownings, all distinguishing marks that would link the aircraft to U.S were removed. The colorful Navy paint schemes were replaced by a French camouflage scheme and the rudders were repainted with the French tri-color rudder stripes. The Curtiss employees worked long and hard to get the job done as quickly as possible.

Gradually all fifty reached Buffalo and the pilots were given their instructions. For the ferry flight, the pilots would become Curtiss employees and be paid $250. 00 plus rail fare back to Buffalo from Halifax, Nova Scotia. Like the SBC-4, they would have to remove anything from their personal effects that would identify them as U.S. Naval personnel.

The pilots were to fly in sections of three, whenever three aircraft were ready to go. The plan was to leave Buffalo, fly to Burlington, Vermont, then on to Augusta, Maine then to Houlton, Maine and finally to Halifax, Nova Scotia. That was the plan; however, because of the idiosyncrasies of international politics, when the aircraft reached the U.S./Canadian border, the pilots were not allowed to fly them over the border. To get around this technicality, the pilots landed at the border crossing at Houlton, and there automobiles and tractors were used to tow the SBC-4s across the border into New Brunswick. This method of border crossing was necessary to meet the requirements of U. S. neutrality laws then in effect. Once over the border, the pilots had to take off from a nearby pasture, then it was on to Halifax where the French aircraft carrier BEARN awaited to transport the SBC-4s to France. The SBC-4s were loaded aboard the BEARN which set to sea on 16 June 1940, escorted by the French cruiser, JEANNE D'ARC. The two ships set out for France, but while at sea, France capitulated to Germany and the little flotilla turned south toward the French West Indies island of Martinique. On this Caribbean island the hastily prepared biplanes were off-loaded and lined-up nose to tail, wing to wing, with canvas coverings over the engines and cockpit canopies.

The SBC-4s were painted in a camouflage scheme consisting of Green and Gray upper-surfaces over Light Blue undersurfaces, although there is no concrete evidence to prove the actual colors used. The aircraft carried the civil registration on the fin and under the wings. (Curtiss via C. Jansson)

Martinique, 1940

Diplomatic wrangling ensued over the fate of the aircraft at Martinique in the aftermath of the fall of France. The French Ambassador informed the Undersecretary of State Sumner Welles, on 30 July 1940, that the French government could not, under the terms of the armistice that it had signed with Germany, return the aircraft to the United States. Welles reiterated to the ambassador that the United States insisted that steps be taken, and reminded him that the Navy had made available a good number of the aircraft "at a time when our own

To comply with U.S. Neutrality Laws, the aircraft could not be flown over the border into Canada. They were landed at Houlton, Maine and pulled across the border by tractor;. They then took-off from a near-by field for the rest of the trip to Halifax, Nova Scotia. (D. Wilson via O. Darcey)

NX-C37 prepares for take-off from the Curtiss factory in Buffalo. French national insignia was applied to the wing upper and lower surfaces and the rudder was painted in the French tri-color. All former U.S. Navy markings were completely removed. (Curtiss via C. Jansson)

defense requirements were uppermost."

The United States government then sent RADM John W. Greenslade to confer with the French High Commissioner for the French West Indies, Admiral Georges Robert, on how the situation could be settled. Robert assured Greenslade, who arrived at his destination on 5 August 1940, that the aircraft on the island (which included SBC-4s) brought to Martinique on board the carrier BEARN and which had been placed ashore at Fort-de-France, would not be transported anywhere. The following day, Admiral Robert declared to the Americans that he was honor-bound to observe the Franco/German armistice, and assured them that no foreign power should fear that the French forces at Martinique would fall into German hands. As proof of his sincerity, he had the aircraft taken off the BEARN and placed ashore, exposed to the elements where, he noted, they would soon deteriorate and become useless through neglect. That afternoon (6 August), Admiral Robert took Admiral Greenslade and the United States Vice Consul at Martinique to inspect the American planes that lay in the open air, "exposed to the elements and not cared for." A later memorandum from the French stated that "the land planes taken ashore at Fort-de-France have been rendered useless by the fact that there is no landing field on the island; that the planes cannot be used on the Carrier BEARN; and that due to the lack of proper shelter and maintenance, the planes will soon deteriorate and thereby be rendered absolutely useless." It was to be an epitaph for the SBCs that had been earmarked for French service, although the matter dragged on into December 1940. Evidence exists that at one point there was consideration given to transferring the aircraft to French Indochina, but that came to naught and they all, including the SBCs, rotted away on the hillside where they had been placed in the Summer of 1940.

Cleveland

While fifty SBC-4s reached Buffalo, only forty-nine completed the mission and five were never loaded aboard the BEARN. The weather at Buffalo had gotten so bad that one of the first SBCs to leave never made it to Burlington on the first leg of the flight. The pilot and air-

Each SBC-4 received a quick customs inspection at the border before being allowed to continue into Canada. The pilot appears to be an enlisted Naval Aviation Pilot (NAP) since he is dressed in dungarees and a Tan flight jacket. (D. Wilson via O. Darcey)

craft were lost between Buffalo and Albany, New York. It was then decided that the pilots would have to wait for better weather before any more take-offs were made. Because of the hectic conditions employed during the time that the SBCs were being prepared for the French, the aircraft radios and instruments were not properly calibrated and became suspect. Therefore, it was decided that further flights would be made under visual flight rules.

Five of the original SBC-4s, destined for France, were not taken aboard the BEARN due to space limitations. These five aircraft remained at Dartmouth, Canada until August of 1940, when they were shipped to England. The five aircraft were NX-C48, 49, 51, 53 and 54. Upon reaching England they were given RAF serial numbers AS467, AS468, AS469, AS470 and

Even though the serial number on this Cleveland Mk I indicates that it is a non-flying instruction airframe, it did take part in a aerial photo session for the RAF Recognition Manual. The aircraft carried standard RAF camouflage on the uppersurfaces with Yellow undersurfaces. (Air Ministry via D. W. Lucabaugh)

NX-C9 is towed across the U.S.-Canadian border. This aircraft appears to carry a third camouflage color on the uppersurfaces, although this has not been proven. (D. Wilson via O. Darcey)

AS471. The RAF assigned the aircraft the name Cleveland Mk I and began evaluating them for possible use.

Eventually the RAF decided the aircraft were not fit for operational use and they were reassigned as instructional airframes and given M serials (which identified the aircraft as non-flying types). One aircraft did fly with the M serials, this was 2669M which was used for a series of photographic missions to pose for photographs for use in RAF recognition manuals.

AS468 (ex-NX-C49) on the ramp at a RAF base during 1940. The British evaluated the SBC and found that they were not fit for operational use in Western Europe. They were used as instructional airframes at mechanic's schools. (Air Ministry via Peter Bowers)

Marine Corps Operations

The SBC-3 had been utilized by only one Marine Corps squadron, VMF-2, which had a single SBC-3 which was used as a squadron hack. The SBC-4; however, was another matter.

The Marine Corps used the XSBC-4 (BuNo 0582), as a staff transport for Headquarters, Marine Corps. This SBC-4 prototype survived until 31 August 1944 when it was stricken from the inventory while serving at NAS Kodiak, Alaska.

The first complete Marine SBC-4 squadron was Marine Observation Squadron One (VMO-1) which began service life during late 1940 with nine Great Lakes BG-1 biplane dive bombers, and a single Grumman J2F-1 biplane amphibian.

During May and June of 1941, VMO-1 started taking deliveries of their first SBC-4s. A total of ten were taken on strength, being delivered to the squadron from various NRABs around the country. BuNo 1478 came from NRAB Kansas City, BuNo 1812 arrived from Squantum, aircraft 1306 came from St. Louis, NRAB Glenview gave up 1319, BuNo 1302 was delivered from NRAB Brooklyn, while BuNo 1823 was flown in from NRAB Atlanta. NRAB Long Beach delivered BuNo 1829, Minneapolis surrendered BuNo 1831 to the Marines and the last, BuNo 1842, came from NRAB New Orleans.

Immediately upon receipt of their SBC-4, the squadron began working up on their new aircraft. Instruments and radios needed replacing, tailhooks had to be installed and all the aircraft had to be repainted in the overall Light Gray camouflage scheme then in use. Since carrier qualifications were to begin on 12 June, mechanics and pilots had to put in long hours to meet the demanding schedule.

After carrier qualifications on 12 June, the squadron spent four days at sea beginning on 17 June. Then they flew to Norfolk for embarcation aboard another carrier.

VMO-1 (Major Thomas C. Green, USMC, commanding) went to sea aboard USS YORKTOWN on 29 June 1941, along with half of the Vought SB2U-3 equipped VMS-1, for neutrality patrol duty, relieving a Navy squadron then re-equipping with Douglas SBDs. The cruise proved largely uneventful until the morning of 1 July when VS-41 (SB2U-2) and VMS-1 scouts reported an unidentified "man of war" twenty-five miles from the task group. YORKTOWN turned into the wind and launched a section of VMO-1 SBC-4s that soon identified the stranger as the American destroyer USS WINSLOW. Interestingly, that interception and identification operation occurred on the same day that the squadron was redesignated

The side code on this SBC-4 identifies it as being assigned to the 1st Marine Air Wing (number 2 aircraft). The aircraft would go on to serve with VB-10 and VS-10 during 1942. (W. T. Larkins)

from VMO-1 to VMO-151.

Ultimately, YORKTOWN returned to Norfolk on 13 July, and the squadron returned to Turner Field, Quantico, Virginia. Other than RANGER (CV-4) operating YORKTOWN's SBC-4 equipped VS-5 (29 May to 8 June 1941), VMO-151's operations with the SBC-4 proved to be the last operational use of the SBC from carriers on the neutrality patrol.

Upon returning to Quantico, the squadron undertook dive-bombing training and participated in the Army/Navy maneuvers from 8 to 30 September 1941. One observer, Lieutenant Colonel Delos C. Emmons, U.S. Army, praised the officers and men of the four Navy and Marine Corps squadrons (three of which, VB-8 and VS-8 from the USS HORNET air group and VMO-151 were equipped with the SBC-4) that participated in the Army's GHQ maneuvers in the Carolinas, lauding them for maintaining the "high standards established by their predecessors in the Louisiana maneuvers." He also praised their "efficiency and. excellent spirit," as they had demonstrated the "fine quality of Naval Aviation, personnel, training and equipment," despite the unfamiliar operating conditions they had encountered.

Once all the high-stress operations ceased, the squadron got down to some serious maintenance work on their SBC-4s. The squadron experienced a rapid turnover in aircraft as 1941 drew to a close. Most of their planes, at this time, were coming from NAS Corpus Christi,

One-Willie-Two on the ramp at Oakland, California during April of 1941. The aircraft was painted in overall Light Gray with White lettering. (Peter Bowers)

Texas. On 6 December 1941, VMO-151 listed an inventory of twelve SBC-4s with three spares.

In the frenzy immediately following the Japanese attack on Pearl Harbor, 7 December 1941, VM0-151 was deployed from MCAS Quantico to NAS North Island, San Diego, California to provide anti-submarine patrol duty in the San Diego-Los Angeles area. On patrol out of NAS Long Beach, and covering an in-bound convoy, 2nd Lieutenant Walter Gregory spied bubbles in the ocean. Checking with home base by radio, reporting what he was seeing and his position, he was given clearance to drop his 500 pound bomb on the suspected enemy submarine, which he did.

Upon returning to Long Beach, he was debriefed and hustled out of sight. It turned out that he had bombed an outlet of the L.A. sewer system, and ever after was known as "Bubbles" Gregory. The squadron returned to MCAS Quantico on 10 January 1942.

After the attack on Pearl Harbor, it was feared the Japanese would continue their advance eastward and it was believed that they would probably strike at Midway, Johnston Island, Palmyra, Samoa or Fiji Island. With this in mind, men, material and aircraft from all the U.S. services were sent as quickly as possible to the many small island outposts in the Central Pacific area.

Shortly after VMO-151 returned to MCAS Quantico, they received a warning order for deployment "beyond the seas." VMO-151 was brought up to strength in pilots by ordering in brand new graduates from flight training, regardless of the type of aircraft they had been

Aircraft Number Two (BuNo 4204) of the Second Marine Air Wing taxies out for another mission. The BuNo and aircraft type lettering on the fin was in one inch White lettering. (F. Shertzer via C. Jansson)

trained on. A number had been trained on fighters and the last three reported in during mid-March 1942, when the squadron's SBC-4s were already in Norfolk being prepared for shipment. These pilots did not fly the SBC-4 until they arrived in Samoa during May.

The wings propellers and tail surfaces had been removed from the SBC-4s and crated. With the upper wing being some thirty-four feet long, this made for a very large crate and a requirement for a transport ship with very large hatches.

The government chartered a Dutch ship, the BRASTAGI, which had been used on the run from Holland to the Dutch East Indies and had very large cargo hatches. A small detachment of enlisted men from VMO-151 under the command of a Marine Gunner were embarked in this ship. They had the only comfortable trip, since the ship still had its civilian crew, was cool and uncrowded, had excellent chow and plenty of good Dutch beer.

The squadron left Norfolk, Virginia on 7 April 1942 along with their brother Marines from VMF-111, a Grumman F4F Wildcat fighter squadron. The squadrons were part of the first large convoy to depart Norfolk since the attack on Pearl Harbor. There were fourteen destroy-

ers and a battleship accompanying the squadrons. The destroyers dropped depth charges on a number of suspected enemy submarines but the convoy never came under attack during the run to Samoa.

The pilots and some of the men of VMO-151 were aboard the USS FULLER (AP-14) and USS MCCAWLEY (AP-10). For all, the trip was a boring, hot and uncomfortable thirty-three days at sea. The commanding officer, Major Green, had planned that, on arrival, the squadron would take the wings and props out of the crates, bolt them back on the SBC-4s, fly the aircraft and live in the crates. This may have been a great scheme on the face of it, but utterly impractical. The crates were built of cheap, low grade knotty pine, lined with tar paper to protect the contents and not designed to stand up under any wear and tear, and certainly not designed as living quarters in a tropical environment. At any rate, this project died a natural death soon after VMO-151 arrived in Samoa.

Disembarking at Pago Pago on 8 May 1942, VMO-151 moved to the recently activated NAS Tutuila, under the command of Major Raymond B. Hurst, USMC. The airstrip was surrounded by heavy jungle growth and the Marines found Tutuila unlike any NAS they had ever experienced, noting particularly the towering mountains that rose directly inshore of the airfield. The ever-present mosquitoes and the prevailing damp, oppressive heat often made

This SBC-4 was totally destroyed after the crew abandoned the aircraft in flight near the California/Mexico border on 5 May 1941. The aircraft had been delivered on 25 February 1941 and had only 49.3 hours on the airframe at the time of the accident. Cause of the crash was engine failure. (Navy via D.W. Lucabaugh)

3-B-11 rests on a work stand after a landing accident at Naval Air Station North Island, San Diego, California. The landing gear truss failed during landing, leading to a collapse of the gear. The damage was not too severe and the aircraft was repaired and placed back into service. (Navy via D.W. Lucabaugh)

sleeping at night quite difficult, while heavy rainfall, often rendered roads impassable. For those who chose to partake of them, recreational activities included fishing, swimming, hiking, tennis, and that staple, movies.

Samoa's air defense consisted of VMF-111 with nineteen F4F-4 Wildcats and VMO-151's twelve SBC-4s. For a short time both squadrons shared the facilities with Scouting Squadron One, Fourteenth Naval District (VS-1-D14) and their seven Vought OS2U-3s, VS-1-D14 had arrived in Samoa on 23 January 1942. This Navy squadron with its OS2Us, Grumman J2F-5s, eight officers and sixty-eight enlisted men were reassigned 100 miles northwest of Samoa to a base, Satapaula, on the British Samoa island of Upolu some thirty days after the arrival of VMO-151 at Tutuila.

Typical of the pilots flying with VMO-151 was Colonel John B. Berteling, USMC, Ret. He recalled it this way, "I have checked my log book, covering the period from 25 May, when I had my first flight in a SBC-4 to 8 December 1942, for a total of about 298.8 hours, logged in twenty-two different SBC-4s, which is about all the aircraft the squadron had at the time. Of this total, 193.2 hours were recorded as patrols or convoy patrol. We had an alert crew of six pilots and six gunners who remained on duty from dawn to dusk every day. I believe these are the ones who flew the anti-submarine patrols around the islands. With this as a constant, there were not many aircraft or flight hours available for training. Maintenance was a real problem, since my log book shows that I flew a number of patrols and some convoy escorts in the Grumman JRF-5 Duck. Some armor was added to protect the engine, and a new pilot's seat was installed, made of armor plate. This made the seat very heavy but they did not

change the bungee cords in the mechanism for adjusting the height of the seat. As a consequence, if you tried to adjust your seat in flight, it was likely to fall to the bottom, and you could barely see out of the cockpit. And it was too heavy to raise without help. Beautiful design. It made landing a bit hairy.

The War Plan to repel the expected Japanese attack was not particularly orthodox. We assumed that the approach of the Japanese invasion force would be detected and shadowed by U.S. submarines. When the force was within range, not radius, of the SBC-4, we would launch all available aircraft, and fly out to the attack. Obviously, on the return flight, the SBCs would run out of gas and ditch in the ocean. Then, the commanding General's PBY-5A would land in the water and pick up the crews. I'm not sure if the plan called for an open ocean take-off, but it certainly was not the sort of plan that inspired confidence in our survival."

VMO-151 had tried for months to update their aircraft. They were, of course, flying the oldest aircraft on active front-line service with the Marine Corps. The best they could get were overhauled SBC-4s from training commands, such as NAS Corpus Christi or San Diego. As early as December of 1941, their SBC-4s had been declared unsatisfactory for long distance flying by the Material Officer for Aircraft at NAS North Island, San Diego. Instead of newer Douglas SBDs, they got reconditioned SBC-4s.

An off-shoot of VMO-151 was VMO-155. They were commissioned at Tutuila on 1 October 1942. VMO-155 consisted of ten SBC-4s and one JRF-5. Their time with the SBC-4 would be short lived and before long they would go on to become the first Marine squadron to fly combat missions from an aircraft carrier. A small section from the squadron took part in the 11 May 1943 invasion of Attu in the Aleutian Islands. Flying from the USS NASSAU

Turtledeck

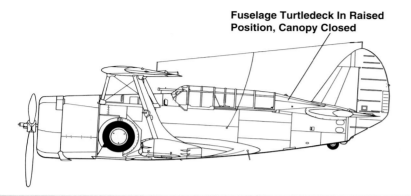

Fuselage Turtledeck In Raised
Position, Canopy Closed

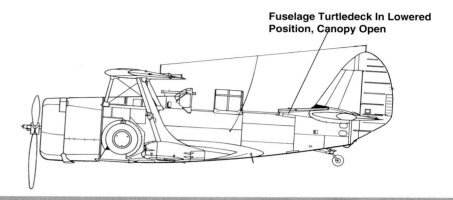

Fuselage Turtledeck In Lowered
Position, Canopy Open

Navy units also participated in the war games. This VB-8 SBC-4 was escorted by a pair
of F4F Wildcat fighters of VMF-111 during the games held in November of 1941.
(Smithsonian Institution via Peter Bowers)

(CVE-16) with F4F-3P Wildcat photographic reconnaissance aircraft.

Marine Scout Bombing Squadron 151 (VMSB-151), formerly VMO-151, remained on Saoma until early 1943, when they finally were re-equipped with SBDs. They had been redesignated as VMSB-151 while still equipped with the old SBC-4s.

Other Marine units that flew the SBC-4 were VMSB-243 and VMSB-244 which flew the SBC-4 during their training cycle in 1942.. Two SBC-4s (BuNos 4219 and 4215) served with

VMF-215 for a few months from June to October of 1942. The squadron had originally been designated VMSB-244 and the unit retained the two SBC-4s for training while re-equipping with fighters. At this time the unit was commanded by Captain James L. Neefus, who had been a division leader in VMF-221 flying Brewster F2A-3s from Midway Island on 10 March 1942. He and three other Marine fighter pilots caught a Japanese Emily flying boat and shot it down. He received the Navy Cross for this mission.

The SBC-4 remained in Marine Corps service almost a full year after the Navy retired theirs.

A SBC-4 of VMO-151 crash landed in a field near Atlanta, Georgia on 19 September 1941. The aircraft carried Red Cross War Games markings on the fin and on the wings. (Navy via D. W. Lucabaugh)

A SBC-4 of VB-8 gets checked out at Columbia Municipal Airport, in Columbia, South Carolina during the joint Army/Navy maneuvers of November 1941. The aircraft carried special war games markings on the fuselage and wings consisting of a Red cross. (Navy/National Archives via D.W. Lucabaugh)

Major Thomas C. Green, Commanding Officer of Marine Observation Squadron 151 (VMO-151) flies this SBC-4 for a photographic sortie during 1941. The rear turtledeck is folded down and there is an external fuel tank on the centerline bomb displacement gear. (R. Arnold via MSGT W. F. Gemeinhardt, USMC, Ret.)

43

This SBC-4 was assigned to the Headqarters Squadron of the First Marine Air WIng during early 1942. At this time there were two SBC-4s assigned, BuNos 4222 and 4225. The aircraft was camouflaged in Non-specular Blue-Gray over Non-specular Light Gray with full rudder stripes. The tail stripes were carried between 5 January 1942 and 15 May 1942, after which time they were deleted. (USMC)

(Left) Two sections of SBC-4s from Marine Observation Squadron 151 (VMO-151) fly in tight formation during 1941. The aircraft are in overall Light Gray with White lettering. All are equipped with an external fuel tank on the centerline bomb rack. The censor has retouched the original photograph, removing the rear guns from all aircraft. (R. Arnold, via M/SGT Gemeinhardt, USMC, Ret.)

A SBC-4 (BuNo 1316) on the transit ramp at Randolph Field, Texas during late 1941. The aircraft originally was assigned to NRAB Seattle during 1939 and was later transferred to Naval Air Station North Island, San Diego, California where it served with Base Air Detachment Two. It is believed that the aircraft was in the process of being transferred to an advanced training unit at NAS Corpus Christi, where it was stricken from the list on 7 July 1943. (Peter Bowers)

Centerline Bomb Displacement Gear Operation

Bomb Stowed

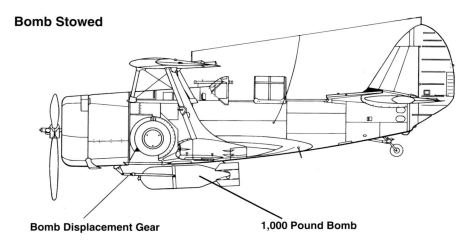

Bomb Displacement Gear

1,000 Pound Bomb

Bomb In The Drop Position

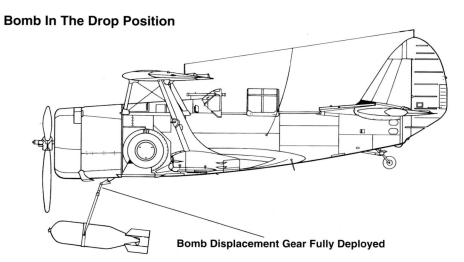

Bomb Displacement Gear Fully Deployed

This SBC-4 of VMO-151 carried the name MISS IRENE on the lower cowling lip in Black. While on Samoa, the aircraft were kept parked in earthen revetments. The bombs on the bomb cart have been fuzed and are ready to load on the Helldivers. (National Archives via R. J. Cressman)

Marine ground crewmen use a bomb cart to transport a 250 pound general purpose bomb to a SBC-4 Helldiver of Marine Observation Squadron 151 (VMO-151) on Samoa Island during September of 1942. The aircraft was camouflaged in Non-specular Blue-Gray over Non-specular Light Gray with Black lettering). (National Archives via R. J. Cressman)

A SBC-4 of VMO-151 on an anti-submarine patrol off the island of Samoa during mid-1942. 151-MO-8 has the turtledeck in the folded position and the gunner has his weapon deployed ready for action. The aircraft is armed with a 500 pound bomb on the centerline bomb displacement gear. There are bomb racks installed under the wings, but they are not fitted with weapons. (B. Porter via MSGT W. F. Gemeinhardt USMC, Ret.)

SBC-4s of Marine Observation Squadron 151 (VMO-151) taxi out to begin their anti-submarine patrols from Tutuila on the Island of Samoa during 1942. VMO-151 was the only squadron to operate the SBC in a combat role. (Colonel R. Bruce Porter USMC, Ret.)

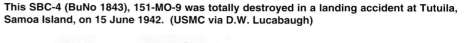

This SBC-4 (BuNo 1843), 151-MO-9 was totally destroyed in a landing accident at Tutuila, Samoa Island, on 15 June 1942. (USMC via D.W. Lucabaugh)

47

A Marine Corps enlisted radioman/gunner mans the air-cooled Browning .30 caliber machine gun in the rear cockpit of a SBC of VMO-151 on Samoa during 1942. The gun has been modified with a ring and bead sight and an armor shield for the gunner. To use the gun, the rear fuselage turtledeck had to be folded down and the rear cockpit canopy was slid forward. This aircraft was 151-MO-11, which was named Miss Irene. (National Archives via R. J. Cressman)

Gunner's Cockpit With Machine Gun In The Stowed Position

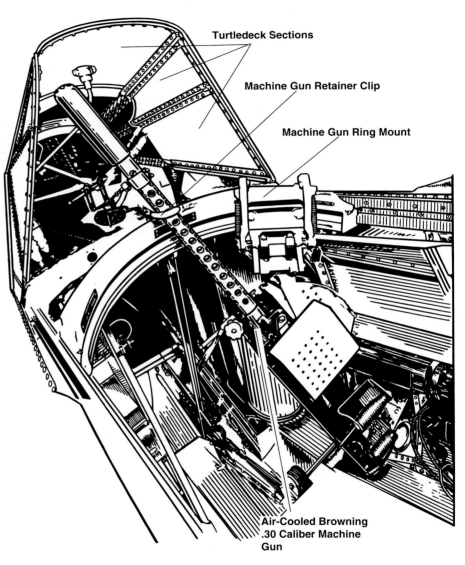

Turtledeck Sections

Machine Gun Retainer Clip

Machine Gun Ring Mount

Air-Cooled Browning .30 Caliber Machine Gun

Aviation Machinist Mates 3rd H.G. Welch (left) and W.E. Magin (right) crank-up one of the last remaining SBC-4s at NAS Corpus Christi, Texas on 1 July 1942. The Marines were still flying the Helldiver operationally, while the Navy had passed the aircraft to training units for use as an advanced trainer. (National Archives via R. J. Cressman)

SBC-3/SBC-4 AIRCRAFT IN OPERATIONAL SERVICE
1937 TO 1943

Squadron Insignia	Carrier	Squadron Designation	1937	1938	1939	1940	1941	1942	1943
	LEXINGTON CV-2	VS-3			2/39 ├───┤ 10/39 LEMON YELLOW TAILS				
(dog insignia)	SARATOGA CV-3	VS-3	9/37 ├───	WHITE TAILS	2/39 ───┤ 10/39	WHITE TAILS	1/41 ├─┤ 4/41 GREY		
(star insignia)	YORKTOWN CV-5	VS-5	7/37 ├───		RED TAILS		1/41 ├─┤ GREY 8/41		
(owl insignia)	ENTERPRISE CV-6	VS-6	10/37 ├───		TRUE BLUE TAILS		1/41 ├─┤ 4/41 GREY		
	LONG ISLAND AVG-1	VS-201					3/41 ├─┤ 6/41 GREY		

SBC-4

Squadron Insignia	Carrier	Squadron Designation	1937	1938	1939	1940	1941	1942	1943
(winged insignia)	LEXINGTON CV-2	VS-2			5/39 ├─── LEMON YELLOW TAILS	───┤ 2/41			
	SARATOGA CV-3	VS-3					2/41 ├─┤ GREY 8/41		
	SARATOGA CV-3	VB-3					4/41 ├─┤ GREY 8/41		
	HORNET CV-8	VS-8					9/41 11/41 GREY ├─┤├─ ↗ 3/42 ─┤CAMOUFLAGE		
	HORNET CV-8	VB-8					9/41 11/41 GREY ├─┤├─ ↗ 3/42 ─┤CAMOUFLAGE		

MARINE SQUADRONS

Squadron Insignia	Carrier	Squadron Designation	1937	1938	1939	1940	1941	1942	1943
(spade insignia)	SAN DIEGO	VMS-2					2/41 3/41 ├─┤ GREY		
	QUANTICO QUANTICO-SAMOA SAMOA	VMO-1* VMO-151** VMSB-151***					*6/41 ├─┤ 7/41 GREY **├─┤GREY ↘	CAMO 9/42 *** ├─┤ CAMO	7/43
	SAMOA	VMO-155						10/42 12/42 ├─┤ CAMO	
	SAN DIEGO/ SANTA BARBARA	VMSB-243						6/42 ├─┤ 12/42 CAMO	
	SAN DIEGO/ SANTA BARBARA	VMSB-244 (VMF-215)						6/42 ├─┤ 12/42 CAMO	

Naval Aviation

From

squadron/signal publications